WINNING

WITH SOLUTION

SELLING

The Secrets to Overcoming Common
Mistakes in Sales Engineering

TALAL GEDEON

WINNING
WITH SOLUTION
SELLING

The Secrets to Overcoming Common Mistakes in Sales Engineering

TALAL GEDEON

This ebook covers topics such as understanding the customer's business and problems, creating solutions that meet their needs, and building long-term relationships.

DESCRIPTION

This ebook covers topics such as understanding the customer's business and problems, creating solutions that meet their needs, and building long-term relationships

Throughout this ebook, you will find THINKING QUESTION's at the end of each chapter

THINKING QUESTION

By taking the time to reflect on this question, Sales Engineers can identify areas for improvement and take steps to become better at handling objections.

FOREWARD

Dear reader,

Congratulations on deciding to take your skills as a Sales Engineer to the next level! Sales Engineering is a difficult and nuanced profession, but with enough practice and dedication, it can also be incredibly rewarding. As with any profession, however, hard work is only part of the formula for success: having proper guidance is critical for developing good habits and furthering your growth. Throughout my career, I have been fortunate to have several mentors who have helped me refine my skills as a Sales Engineer; encouraged my growth more broadly as a sales professional; and, most importantly, pointed me in the right direction when I was starting out. Without that foundation, I wouldn't be half the Sales Engineer I am today. To that last point, I am delighted that my dear friend Talal has decided to help other current and aspiring Sales Engineers learn how to refine their craft. With this e-book, Talal has written the type of guide I wish I'd had when I began my career!

Prior to joining my Sales Engineering team, Talal developed his technical and customer-facing skills by working first as a Sales Development Representative, and later as a Sales Engineer within the IoT space. When I first met Talal, he immediately wowed me with his extensive technical knowledge, refined presentation skills, and strong presence in meetings. Moreover, I was impressed by his wealth of self-produced online content to help others stay up to date on industry trends, particularly his videos on LinkedIn. It's rare to come across people so passionate not just about improving their own skills, but also about helping others with their professional growth. That personality naturally lends itself to being a skilled and effective Sales Engineer, as the role of an SE is largely to teach prospective customers and improve their understanding of your platform or product. Talal excelled as a trusted member of my team and has continued to share his talents as a Sales Engineer and LinkedIn Learning Instructor. Rest assured, you are in great hands with Talal as you continue your growth as a Sales Engineer.

In the coming chapters, you will learn many of the fundamental skills for being an effective Sales Engineer. In addition to teaching you the basics—such as how to be an effective listener, how to deliver effective presentations, and how to communicate effectively—Talal will walk you through some of the most frequently made mistakes in Sales Engineering and how to overcome them. As you learn about these common pitfalls and strategies for navigating them, you will become more aware of your own tendencies and learn to think more critically about how you conduct yourself, both in meetings with prospective customers and more generally. With this newfound knowledge, you will be able to more easily self-reflect; engage effectively with prospective customers; and ultimately, sell larger and better deals. I hope you get everything you're looking for out of this book and wish you luck with your ongoing Sales Engineering journey!

ABOUT THE AUTHOR

I am a Sales Engineer with experience in selling complex technical solutions in the Internet of Things (IoT) and Big Data industries along with being a Linkedin Instructor for "How Tech Drives Sustainability."

Due to my experience, I have developed an understanding of the importance of solution selling in today's market.

My focus has been on customer-facing conversations, optimizing customer solutions, and troubleshooting technical issues. However, when I first embarked on this journey as a Sales Engineer, I faced many challenges in learning how to become a successful Sales Engineer.

In this book, I will be sharing the top lessons and insights that I have learned and providing valuable information for anyone looking to expand their skills in Sales Engineering and successfully sell complex products and services.

ACKNOWLEDGMENTS

I'd like to say thank you to

Calvin Jepson,
For giving me the opportunity to become the first sales engineer at
Particle

Mingo Sanchez,
For proofreading and editing the manuscript. Along with being a
friend and a mentor

TABLE OF CONTENTS

INTRODUCTION

Welcome to 'Winning with Solution Selling: The Secrets to Overcoming Common Mistakes in Sales Engineering.' In this e-book, we will explore the art and science of selling complex technical products and services.

The world of sales is constantly evolving, and the role of a Sales Engineer is no exception. You may have come across various terms such as pre-Sales Engineer, Solutions Architect, Solutions Engineer, and Solutions Consultant, but ultimately, they all refer to the same thing - selling complex technical products.

In this e-book, we will dive into the intricacies of understanding your customer's business and problems, creating solutions that meet their needs, and building long-term relationships. Whether new to the field or a seasoned sales professional, this e-book will provide valuable insights and strategies to help you excel in your role. Let's begin!

UNDERSTAND THE CUSTOMER'S NEEDS AND PAIN POINTS

Understanding the customer's needs and pain points is a crucial aspect of the sales process. As a Sales Engineer, it's your responsibility to identify and address the customer's specific needs and pain points to provide them with effective solutions. However, this can be a challenging task, and it's easy to make mistakes.

In this chapter, we will discuss some of the most common mistakes Sales Engineers make when trying to understand the customer's needs and pain points and provide strategies for avoiding them. By understanding the customer's needs and pain points, you will be able to build stronger relationships with customers, close more deals, and ultimately be more successful in your role.

Below are the top 5 mistakes Sales Engineers make when trying to understand the customer's needs and pain points:

1. **Not asking enough questions or not listening actively to the customer**: It's essential to actively listen to the customer and ask follow-up questions to gain a deeper understanding of their needs and challenges.

2. **Not conducting proper research or gathering enough information:** It's important to gather information from various sources, such as customer surveys, interviews, and market research, to get a clear and accurate understanding of the customer's needs and pain points.

3. **Not tailoring your approach to the specific customer:** Each customer is unique and may have different needs and pain points, so it's important to tailor your approach and solutions to address those specific needs.

4. **Focusing too much on the features of the product or service rather than the benefits it can provide to the customer:** It's important to communicate how the product or service can address the customer's specific needs and pain points.

5. **Not taking the time to understand the customer's business and their goals truly:** Leads to a lack of understanding of the customer's needs and pain points, and it's also important to understand their budget and decision-making process.

How to overcome these top 5 mistakes:

1. **To overcome the mistake of not asking enough questions or not listening actively to the customer:** It's essential to make a conscious effort to actively listen to the customer and ask follow-up questions. This can be achieved by taking notes during the conversation, repeating key points back to the customer, and asking open-ended questions that encourage the customer to share more information.

2. **To overcome the mistake of not conducting proper research or gathering enough information:** It's important to establish a research plan and gather information from various sources. This may include customer surveys, interviews, and market research. Additionally, it's important to stay up-to-date on industry trends and new technologies that may affect the customer's needs and pain points.

3. **To overcome the mistake of not tailoring your approach to the specific customer:** It's important to take the time to understand each customer's unique needs and pain points. This can be achieved by conducting research on the customer and their industry and asking questions during the sales process to gather more information. Additionally, it's important to adjust your approach and solutions to address the specific needs of each customer.

4. **To overcome the mistake of focusing too much on the features of the product or service rather than the**

benefits it can provide to the customer: It's important to focus on the value that your product or service can provide to the customer. This may include reducing costs, increasing efficiency, or solving specific pain points. Additionally, it's important to clearly communicate how your product or service can address the customer's specific needs and pain points.

5. **To overcome the mistake of not taking the time to truly understand the customer's business and their goals:** It's important to take the time to research the customer and their industry and understand their specific goals and budget. This can be achieved by conducting customer interviews, researching the customer's industry, and understanding their decision-making process. Additionally, it's important to stay in touch with the customer and understand any changes in their needs or pain points.

In conclusion, understanding the customer's needs and pain points is a crucial aspect of the sales process. However, it can be easy for Sales Engineers to make mistakes. By avoiding common mistakes such as not asking enough questions, not conducting proper research, not tailoring your approach to the specific customer, focusing too much on features rather than benefits, and not taking the time to understand the customer's business and their goals truly, Sales Engineers can provide effective solutions to the customer's needs and pain points.

THINKING QUESTION

"How can I improve my approach when it comes to understanding my customer's needs and pain points?"

BUILD STRONG RELATIONSHIPS WITH CUSTOMERS AND OTHER STAKEHOLDERS

Building strong relationships with customers and other stakeholders is an essential aspect of the sales process. As a Sales Engineer, it's important to understand the customer's decision-making process and to be able to effectively communicate with and influence each stakeholder. Additionally, providing excellent customer service, following up with customers regularly, and being able to empathize with the customer are all important elements of building strong relationships. However, this can be a challenging task, and it's easy to make mistakes.

In this chapter, we will discuss some of the most common mistakes Sales Engineers make when trying to build strong relationships with customers and other stakeholders and provide strategies for avoiding them. By building strong relationships with customers and other stakeholders, you will be able to close more deals, increase customer loyalty, and ultimately be more successful in your role.

Top 5 mistakes Sales Engineers do when building relationships with customers:

1. **Not understanding the customer's decision-making process:** It's important to understand who is involved in the decision-making process, and how to effectively communicate with and influence each stakeholder. Failing to understand the customer's decision-making process can lead to delays in closing deals and can make it more difficult to build a strong relationship.

2. **Not being able to empathize with the customer:** Building a strong relationship requires understanding the customer's perspective and being able to put oneself in their shoes. Failing to empathize with the customer can lead to misunderstandings and can make it more difficult to build trust and credibility.

3. **Not providing excellent customer service:** It's important to go above and beyond to ensure customer satisfaction and build loyalty. Failing to provide excellent customer service can lead to dissatisfaction and can make it harder to build a strong relationship.

4. **Not following up with customers regularly:** By not following up with customers regularly, it's easy to miss out on potential opportunities and lose touch with the customer. Failing to maintain regular communication with customers can lead to a loss of trust and can make it harder to build a strong relationship.

5. **Not being able to effectively communicate with customers and stakeholders:** Being able to communicate effectively, both verbally and in writing, is crucial for building strong relationships with customers and other stakeholders. Failing to communicate effectively can lead to misunderstandings and can make it more difficult to build trust and credibility.

How to overcome these top 5 mistakes:

1. **To overcome the mistake of not understanding the customer's decision-making process:** It's important to make a conscious effort to gather information about the customer's decision-making process. This can include researching the customer's company, their role in the company, and their decision-making authority. Additionally, it's important to understand their individual communication preferences and to tailor your approach accordingly.

2. **To overcome the mistake of not being able to empathize with the customer:** It's important to make a conscious effort to understand the customer's perspective and to put oneself in their shoes. This can be achieved by actively listening to the customer, asking follow-up questions, and understanding their specific needs and pain points.

3. **To overcome the mistake of not providing excellent customer service:** It's important to make a conscious effort to exceed customer expectations and to provide clear and accurate information. Additionally, it's important to be responsive to customer needs and to be proactive in solving customer problems.

4. **To overcome the mistake of not following up with customers regularly:** It's important to establish a communication schedule and to make a conscious effort to stay in touch with customers. This can include sending follow-up emails, making regular phone calls, or scheduling face-to-face meetings.

5. **To overcome the mistake of not being able to communicate with customers and stakeholders effectively:** It's important to make a conscious effort to improve communication skills. This can include practicing effective communication techniques, such as active listening, clear and concise writing, and handling objections. Additionally, it's important to be aware of cultural differences and to tailor your communication style accordingly.

In conclusion, building strong relationships with customers and other stakeholders is an essential aspect of the sales process. However, it can be easy for Sales Engineers to make mistakes when trying to build these relationships. By avoiding common mistakes such as not understanding the customer's decision-making process, not being able to empathize with the customer, not providing excellent customer service, not following up with customers regularly, and not being able to effectively communicate with customers and stakeholders, Sales Engineers can build stronger relationships with customers, increase customer loyalty, and ultimately be more successful in their role. Achieving this takes time, effort, and continuous work to maintain.

THINKING QUESTION:

"What can I do to understand my customer's decision-making process better, build stronger relationships and provide excellent customer service?"

COMMUNICATE EFFECTIVELY, BOTH VERBALLY AND IN WRITING

Communicating effectively, both verbally and in writing, is a crucial aspect of the sales process. As a Sales Engineer, it's important to be able to clearly articulate the value of the product or service, respond to customer inquiries promptly, handle objections effectively, present information effectively, and adapt communication style to different audiences. However, it can be easy to make mistakes when trying to communicate effectively.

In this chapter, we will discuss some of the most common mistakes Sales Engineers make when trying to communicate effectively and the impact these mistakes can have on the sales process. By understanding these mistakes and learning to communicate effectively, Sales Engineers can build stronger relationships with customers, close more deals, and ultimately be more successful in their role.

Below are the top 5 mistakes Sales Engineers do when communicating with customers:

1. **Not being able to clearly articulate the value proposition:** The ability to clearly communicate the value of the product or service to the customer is an important aspect of the sales process. It is crucial for Sales Engineers to be able to effectively communicate the unique features, benefits, and advantages of the product or service in order to differentiate it from competitors and demonstrate its value to the customer.

2. **Not being able to respond to customer inquiries promptly:** Responding to customer inquiries promptly is essential for building trust and credibility with the customer. Failing to respond to customer inquiries promptly can lead to frustration on the customer's part and can damage the relationship.

3. **Not being able to handle objections effectively:** Objections are a normal part of the sales process, but being able to effectively handle objections is crucial for closing deals. Failing to address or overcome objections can lead to lost opportunities and can damage the relationship with the customer.

4. **Not being able to effectively present information:** Effective presentation is an important aspect of the sales process, it is crucial for Sales Engineers to be able to effectively present information, both verbally and in writing, to the customer. This includes the ability to

24

clearly and concisely communicate the value of the product or service, to use appropriate language and terminology, and to create effective visual aids.

5. **Not being able to adapt communication style to different audiences:** Understanding and adapting communication style to different audiences is important for building strong relationships and closing deals. Sales Engineers should be able to adapt their communication style depending on the audience, whether it's a C-level executive or technical lead.

How to overcome these top 5 mistakes:

1. **To overcome the mistake of not being able to articulate the value proposition clearly:** It's important to spend time researching and understanding the product or service, as well as the market and the competition. This will give you the knowledge and insight you need to communicate effectively the unique features, benefits, and advantages of the product or service. Additionally, practice and rehearse your pitch, and tailor it to the specific customer.

2. **To overcome the mistake of not being able to respond to customer inquiries in a timely manner:** It's important to establish a system for tracking and responding to customer inquiries. This can include setting up a system for scheduling follow-up calls or emails and training team members on how to respond

to customer inquiries effectively. Additionally, make an effort to be available and responsive to customer needs, and set clear communication expectations.

3. **To overcome the mistake of not being able to handle objections effectively:** It's important to anticipate and prepare for potential objections in advance. This can include researching and understanding the customer's specific needs and pain points and developing effective responses to common objections. Additionally, be open to feedback and be willing to address and overcome objections professionally.

4. **To overcome the mistake of not being able to present information effectively:** It's important to practice and rehearse presentations in advance and to use effective visual aids, such as charts, graphs, and images, to help communicate key points. Additionally, be aware of your tone, body language, and pace when presenting.

5. **To overcome the mistake of not being able to adapt communication style to different audiences:** It's important to research and understand the specific needs and communication preferences of different audiences. This can include understanding cultural differences and tailoring your communication style accordingly. Additionally, be aware of your audience's level of technical expertise and use appropriate language and terminology when communicating with them.

In conclusion, communicating effectively, both verbally and in writing, is a crucial aspect of the sales process. However, it can be easy for Sales Engineers to make mistakes when trying to communicate effectively. By understanding common mistakes such as not being able to clearly articulate the value proposition, not being able to respond to customer inquiries promptly, not being able to handle objections effectively, not being able to present information effectively, and not being able to adapt communication style to different audiences, Sales Engineers can improve their communication skills and ultimately be more successful in their role. Remember that effective communication takes practice and effort to master, and it's a continuous process that needs improvement.

THINKING QUESTION:

"How can I improve my communication skills better to articulate the value of my product or service, handle objections and adapt to different audiences?"

STAY UP TO DATE ON INDUSTRY TRENDS AND NEW TECHNOLOGIES

Staying up-to-date on industry trends and new technologies is an important aspect of the sales process. As a Sales Engineer, it's important to be informed about the latest developments in your industry to be able to effectively communicate the value of your product or service to customers and to be able to differentiate it from competitors. However, it can be easy to fall behind on industry trends and new technologies.

In this chapter, we will discuss some of the most common mistakes Sales Engineers make when trying to stay up-to-date on industry trends and new technologies and the impact these mistakes can have on the sales process. By understanding these mistakes and learning to stay up-to-date on industry trends and new technologies, Sales Engineers can improve their ability to communicate the value of their product or service, close more deals, and ultimately be more successful in their role.

Below are the top 5 mistakes Sales Engineers make when staying up to date on industry trends:

1. **Not staying informed about industry trends and new technologies:** Sales Engineers need to stay informed about industry trends and new technologies to be able to effectively communicate the value of their product or service to customers and to be able to differentiate it from competitors.

2. **Not attending industry events and conferences:** Attending industry events and conferences is an important way for Sales Engineers to stay informed about industry trends and new technologies.

3. **Not reading industry publications and following relevant social media accounts:** Keeping up with industry publications and following relevant social media accounts is a good way for Sales Engineers to stay informed about industry trends and new technologies.

4. **Not actively seeking out new learning opportunities:** Actively seeking out new learning opportunities, such as training courses, webinars, or workshops, is a good way for Sales Engineers to stay informed about industry trends and new technologies.

5. **Not taking the time to research and understand the competition:** It is important for Sales Engineers to research and understand the competition to be able to

effectively communicate their own value proposition and differentiate it from others. This includes understanding the strengths and weaknesses of competitors, as well as their pricing, product offerings, and sales strategies. By staying up-to-date on the competitive landscape, Sales Engineers can better anticipate and respond to customer needs and objections, ultimately increasing the chances of closing a sale.

How to overcome these top 5 mistakes:

1. **To overcome the mistake of not staying informed about industry trends and new technologies:** It's important to set aside dedicated time each week or month to read industry publications, attend industry events and conferences, and follow relevant social media accounts. Additionally, try to stay informed about new technologies and industry trends by actively seeking new learning opportunities such as training courses, webinars, or workshops.

2. **To overcome the mistake of not attending industry events and conferences:** It's important to plan to attend a certain number of events and conferences each year and to research relevant events and schedule them in advance. This can include setting a budget for attending events, researching relevant events and

conferences, and making a schedule to attend these events. Virtual events also offer a convenient way to stay updated on industry trends and network with peers. It's important to make a plan to attend a certain number of virtual events and webinars each year and. This can help you stay informed and connected with others in your industry without the need for travel.

3. **To overcome the mistake of not reading industry publications and following relevant social media accounts:** It's important to set aside dedicated time each week or month to read industry publications and follow relevant social media content. Additionally, create a list of relevant publications and social media accounts to follow and check for updates regularly.

4. **To overcome the mistake of not actively seeking new learning opportunities:** It's important to plan to attend a certain number of training courses, webinars, or workshops each year. This can include setting a budget for attending these events, researching relevant learning opportunities, and making a schedule to attend these events.

5. **To overcome the mistake of not taking the time to research and understand new technologies:** It's important to set aside dedicated time each week or month to research and understand new technologies. Additionally, make an effort to stay informed about

new technologies by actively seeking out new learning opportunities.

6. **To overcome the mistake of not taking the time to research and understand the competition:** It's important to set aside dedicated time each week or month to research and understand the competition. This includes understanding the strengths and weaknesses of competitors, as well as their pricing, product offerings, and sales strategies.

In conclusion, staying up-to-date on industry trends and new technologies is an important aspect of the sales process. By staying informed about the latest developments in your industry, Sales Engineers can improve their ability to communicate the value of their product or service to customers and to differentiate it from competitors. However, it can be easy to make mistakes when trying to stay up-to-date on industry trends and new technologies. By understanding common mistakes such as not staying informed about industry trends and new technologies, not attending industry events and conferences, not reading industry publications and following relevant social media accounts, not actively seeking out new learning opportunities, and not taking the time to research and understand new technologies, Sales Engineers can improve their ability to stay up-to-date on industry trends and new technologies. Remember that staying up-to-date on industry trends and new technologies is an ongoing process that requires dedication and effort.

THINKING QUESTION

"What steps can I take to stay up-to-date on industry trends and new technologies that will be most effective for me?"

BE ABLE TO DEMONSTRATE AND EXPLAIN PRODUCTS OR SERVICES EFFECTIVELY

Being able to demonstrate and explain products or services effectively is an essential aspect of the sales process. As a Sales Engineer, your ability to clearly and effectively demonstrate the product or service to the customer and effectively communicate its value and features can be the key to closing deals and building strong customer relationships. However, it can be easy to make mistakes when trying to demonstrate and explain products or services effectively.

In this chapter, we will discuss some of the most common mistakes Sales Engineers make when trying to demonstrate and explain products or services effectively, and the impact these mistakes can have on the sales process. By understanding these mistakes and learning how to demonstrate and explain products or services effectively, Sales Engineers can improve their ability to close deals, build strong relationships with customers, and ultimately be more successful in their role.

Below are the top 5 mistakes Sales Engineers make when demonstrating or explaining products and services:

1. **Not being able to clearly and effectively demonstrate the product or service:** Sales Engineers need to be able to clearly and effectively demonstrate the product or service to the customer in order to communicate its value and features effectively.

2. **Not understanding the customer's needs and pain points:** Sales Engineers need to understand the customer's needs and pain points to tailor the demonstration of the product or service to their specific needs.

3. **Not being able to effectively explain the technical aspects of the product or service:** Sales Engineers need to be able to effectively explain the technical aspects of the product or service, such as features and functionality, to effectively communicate its value and differentiators to the customer.

4. **Not being able to handle and address objections during the demonstration effectively:** Sales Engineers need to be able to effectively handle and address any objections that may arise during the demonstration to effectively communicate the value of the product or service.

5. **Not being able to follow up and close the sale after the demonstration effectively:** Sales Engineers need to be able to effectively follow up and close the sale after the demonstration in order to communicate the value of the product or service effectively and to convert the customer into a paying customer.

How to overcome these top 5 mistakes:

1. **To overcome the mistake of not being able to clearly and effectively demonstrate the product or service:** It's important for Sales Engineers to practice and familiarize themselves with the product or service before the demonstration. Sales Engineers should also take the time to understand the customer's needs and pain points and tailor the demonstration accordingly. Additionally, Sales Engineers should use visual aids and examples to help clearly communicate the value and features of the product or service, for example, record yourself, then watch and analyze your recordings. Another way to do this is live practice with a colleague for a mock scenario.

2. **To overcome the mistake of not understanding the customer's needs and pain points:** Sales Engineers should conduct research on the customer before the demonstration, ask questions during the demonstration and actively listen to the customer's

needs and pain points, and tailor the demonstration to address those specific needs.

3. **To overcome the mistake of not being able to explain the technical aspects of the product or service effectively:** Sales Engineers should research and understand the technical aspects of the product or service before the demonstration and use simple, easy-to-understand language to explain these technical aspects to nontechnical customers. When speaking with experts or highly technical people, use appropriate sophisticated language.

4. **To overcome the mistake of not being able to effectively handle and address objections during the demonstration:** Sales Engineers should anticipate and prepare for common objections and practice effectively addressing those objections. Additionally, Sales Engineers should actively listen to and address the customer's concerns and objections during the demonstration.

5. **To overcome the mistake of not being able to follow up and close the sale after the demonstration effectively:** Sales Engineers should establish a clear follow-up plan, including a specific timeline for following up with the customer, and prepare closing techniques and arguments. Additionally, Sales Engineers should actively listen to the customer's

concerns and objections and address them during the follow-up process.

In conclusion, being able to effectively demonstrate and explain products or services is an essential aspect of the sales process. Understanding and addressing common mistakes such as not being able to clearly and effectively demonstrate the product or service, not understanding the customer's needs and pain points, not being able to effectively explain the technical aspects of the product or service, not being able to effectively handle and address objections during the demonstration, and not being able to effectively follow-up and close the sale after the demonstration can greatly improve Sales Engineers' ability to close deals, build strong relationships with customers, and ultimately be more successful in their role.

THINKING QUESTION

"What specific steps can I take to improve my ability to effectively demonstrate and explain products or services to customers?"

BE ABLE TO HANDLE OBJECTIONS AND OVERCOME THEM

Handling objections is an important part of the sales process. As a Sales Engineer, your ability to effectively handle and overcome objections can be the key to closing deals and building strong customer relationships. However, it can be easy to make mistakes when trying to handle objections.

In this chapter, we will discuss some of the most common mistakes Sales Engineers make when trying to handle objections and the impact these mistakes can have on the sales process. By understanding these mistakes and learning how to effectively handle objections, Sales Engineers can improve their ability to close deals, build strong relationships with customers, and ultimately be more successful in their role.

Below are the top 5 mistakes Sales Engineers make in objection handling:

1. **Not actively listening to the customer's objections:** Failing to actively listen to the customer's objections can lead to a lack of understanding of the customer's

concerns, which can make it more difficult to address and overcome them. It also can create an impression of not caring about the customer's needs and concerns.

2. **Not being prepared to handle objections:** Sales Engineers should anticipate and prepare for common objections in order to be able to effectively address them when they arise. Failing to do so can lead to confusion and delay in the sales process and can make it more difficult to overcome objections and close the sale.

3. **Not being able to address the customer's objections effectively:** Sales Engineers should be able to effectively address the customer's objections and present counterarguments that effectively communicate the value of the product or service. Failing to do so can lead to the customer remaining unconvinced and can make it more difficult to close the sale.

4. **Failing to follow up on objections:** Sales Engineers should follow up on objections to ensure that they have been fully addressed and to prevent them from becoming roadblocks in closing the sale. Failing to follow up can lead to the customer remaining unconvinced and can make it more difficult to close the sale.

5. **Being defensive when addressing objections:** When addressing objections, Sales Engineers should avoid

being defensive and instead approach them with a solution-focused mindset. Being defensive can create a negative impression and can make it more difficult to overcome objections and close the sale.

How to overcome these top 5 mistakes:

1. **To overcome not actively listening to the customer's objections:** Sales Engineers should practice active listening techniques such as repeating or paraphrasing the customer's objections to confirm understanding, asking follow-up questions to gain more insight into the customer's concerns and making sure to fully understand the customer's concerns before addressing them. It is also important to allow the customer to fully express their objections and not interrupt or try to refute them immediately.

2. **To overcome not being prepared to handle objections:** Sales Engineers should anticipate and prepare for common objections by researching the product or service and its competition, understanding the customer's needs and pain points and rehearsing potential objections and responses. This can involve understanding the customer's decision-making process, budget, and any concerns they may have about the product or service.

3. **To overcome not being able to address the customer's objections effectively:** Sales Engineers should be able

to provide clear and compelling counterarguments that demonstrate how the product or service addresses the customer's specific needs and pain points. This involves focusing on the customer's needs and using examples and evidence to support counterarguments. It's also important to address the customer's objections in a way tailored to the specific customer and their needs.

4. **To overcome failing to follow up on objections:** Sales Engineers should make sure to follow up with the customer after addressing their objections to ensure that they have been fully addressed and to prevent them from becoming roadblocks in closing the sale. This can involve scheduling a follow-up call or meeting to discuss the objections and the proposed solutions.

5. **To overcome being defensive when addressing objections:** Sales Engineers should approach objections with a solution-focused mindset, maintain a positive attitude and avoid getting defensive or argumentative when addressing the customer's objections. This can involve acknowledging the customer's concerns and working with them to find a solution that addresses those concerns.

In conclusion, handling objections is an important part of the sales process for Sales Engineers. By understanding common mistakes Sales Engineers make when trying to handle objections and learning how to handle and overcome objections effectively, Sales Engineers can improve their ability to close deals, build strong relationships with customers, and ultimately be more successful in their role. Some of the most common mistakes include not actively listening to the customer's objections, being unprepared to handle objections, not being able to effectively address the customer's objections, failing to follow up on objections, and being defensive when addressing objections. By understanding and learning how to overcome these mistakes, Sales Engineers can improve their ability to handle objections and close deals.

THINKING QUESTION

"What are some common objections that I encounter in my sales process, and how have I prepared to handle them effectively?"

BE ABLE TO DEVELOP AND DELIVER EFFECTIVE PRESENTATIONS

In this chapter, we will explore the most common mistakes Sales Engineers made when developing and delivering effective presentations. We will examine how a lack of tailoring to the specific audience, poor use of visual aids, lack of practice, inappropriate language and terminology, and poor handling of Q&A sessions can negatively impact the sales process and make it more difficult to close deals. We will also provide strategies for overcoming these mistakes and delivering successful presentations that effectively communicate the product's or service's value to the customer.

Below are the top 5 mistakes Sales Engineers make when developing and delivering effective presentations:

1. **Not tailoring the presentation to the specific audience:** Sales Engineers should tailor their presentations to the specific audience by understanding their needs, pain points, and decision-

making process. This includes understanding their technical expertise level, industry, and goals. Failing to tailor the presentation to the specific audience can lead to a lack of engagement and interest and make it more difficult to close the sale.

2. **Not effectively using visual aids:** Sales Engineers should use visual aids such as slides, diagrams, and images to effectively communicate the key points of the presentation and make it more engaging for the audience. The visual aids should be clear and easy to understand, and they should be used to support the main points of the presentation, not as a distraction. Failing to use visual aids effectively can lead to a lack of engagement and interest from the audience and make it more difficult to communicate the value of the product or service.

3. **Not practicing the presentation beforehand:** Sales Engineers should practice the presentation to ensure that it flows smoothly and that they are comfortable delivering it. This includes rehearsing the timing, delivery, and use of visual aids. Failing to practice can lead to a lack of confidence and engagement from the audience, making it more difficult to close the sale.

4. **Not using appropriate language and terminology:** Sales Engineers should use appropriate language and terminology that is easily understood by the audience. This includes using industry-specific terms and

avoiding technical jargon that may be confusing to the audience. Failing to use appropriate language and terminology can lead to confusion and a lack of engagement from the audience and make it more difficult to communicate the product's or service's value.

5. **Not effectively handling Q&A session:** Sales Engineers should be able to effectively handle the Q&A session by answering questions clearly and confidently. This includes being prepared for potential questions, staying calm under pressure, and being able to redirect the conversation if necessary. Failing to handle the Q&A session effectively can lead to a lack of credibility and trust from the audience and can make it more difficult to close the sale.

How to overcome these top 5 mistakes:

1. **When tailoring the presentation to a specific audience:** Sales Engineers must research and understand their needs, pain points, and decision-making process. This can include understanding their level of technical expertise, their industry, and their goals. To do this, Sales Engineers can talk to the customer, conduct market research, and identify key stakeholders.

2. **Using visual aids such as slides, diagrams, and images:** Using visual aids can be an effective way to

communicate the key points of the presentation and make it more engaging for the audience. However, it's important to ensure that the visual aids are clear and easy to understand, and used to support the main points of the presentation rather than as a distraction. Additionally, it's important to avoid having too dense or wordy slides, as it can lead to the audience focusing on reading rather than paying attention to what's being said. The slides should summarize the talking points, but the spoken content should provide more detailed information.

3. **Practicing the presentation beforehand:** Is crucial to ensure that it flows smoothly and that the Sales Engineer is comfortable delivering it. This includes rehearsing the timing, delivery, and use of visual aids. Sales Engineers can practice in front of colleagues or a mirror to get feedback.

4. **Using appropriate language and terminology that is easily understood by the audience is important:** This includes using industry-specific terms and avoiding technical jargon that may confuse the audience. Sales Engineers can identify the target audience by researching the language and terminology they use during discovery calls and incorporating these into their presentation. This will help to ensure that the audience understands and feels engaged with the content.

5. **Effectively handling the Q&A session:** Can be achieved by being prepared for potential questions, staying calm under pressure, and being able to redirect the conversation if necessary. Sales Engineers can anticipate potential questions and prepare answers, stay calm by taking deep breaths, and redirect the conversation if the question is not relevant to the presentation. Additionally, it's important to actively listen to the audience and address any concerns or objections they may have.

In conclusion, developing and delivering effective presentations is an important skill for Sales Engineers. The most common mistakes in this area include not tailoring the presentation to the specific audience, not effectively using visual aids, not practicing the presentation beforehand, not using appropriate language and terminology, and not effectively handling the Q&A session. By understanding these mistakes and taking steps to overcome them, Sales Engineers can improve their ability to effectively communicate the value of their product or service to the customer.

THINKING QUESTION

How can I continue to improve my ability to develop and deliver effective presentations?

BE ABLE TO WORK WELL IN A TEAM

In this chapter, we will delve into the most common mistakes Sales Engineers make when working in a team, and explore ways to overcome them. Effective communication, active participation, willingness to help and share information, the ability to handle conflicts and challenges, and taking responsibility for team successes and failures are all crucial components of working well in a team. By understanding these common mistakes and learning how to overcome them, Sales Engineers will be better equipped to work effectively with their team and achieve success in the sales process.

Below are the top 5 mistakes Sales Engineers make when working in a team:

1. **Not effectively communicating with team members:** Sales Engineers should be able to effectively communicate with team members to ensure that everyone is on the same page and that tasks are being completed efficiently. Failing to effectively communicate

can lead to confusion and delays in the sales process and can negatively impact team dynamics.

2. **Not actively participating in team meetings:** Sales Engineers should actively participate in team meetings to stay informed about team progress and to provide input and feedback. Failing to participate actively can lead to a lack of understanding of team goals and negatively impact team dynamics.

3. **Not being willing to help others or share information:** Sales Engineers should be willing to help others and share information to ensure that the team is working efficiently and effectively. Failing to do so can lead to a lack of trust and cooperation among team members and can negatively impact team dynamics.

4. **Not being able to handle conflicts or challenges within the team:** Sales Engineers should be able to handle conflicts or challenges within the team professionally and constructively. Failing to do so can lead to a breakdown in team dynamics and can negatively impact the sales process.

5. **Not taking responsibility for team successes and failures:** As a Sales Engineer, it's important to take ownership of both the successes and failures of the team to improve performance and efficiency continuously. Failing to do so, it can create a lack of accountability and negatively affect team morale and dynamics.

How to overcome these top 5 mistakes:

1. **To overcome not effectively communicating with team members:** Sales Engineers should take time to understand their team members' communication preferences and needs, actively seek out and provide feedback, and make sure to articulate expectations and goals. This can be done by setting up regular team meetings, creating clear and concise agendas, and encouraging open and honest communication. Additionally, it's helpful for Sales Engineers to provide a written overview of their preferred communication style, including working hours and preferred mode of communication.

2. **To overcome not actively participating in team meetings:** Sales Engineers should prioritize attending all team meetings, come prepared with questions and insights, and actively contribute to discussions and decision-making. This can be done by setting aside time to review the agenda and materials before the meeting, actively engaging in the discussion, and providing constructive feedback and suggestions.

3. **To overcome not being willing to help others or share information:** Sales Engineers should make an effort to be supportive of team members, offer assistance when needed, and actively share relevant information with team members. This can be done by creating an open and collaborative work environment, encouraging knowledge sharing, and recognizing and rewarding team members for their contributions. Additionally, by

helping your team members, they will be more inclined to reciprocate and offer assistance.

4. **To overcome being unable to handle conflicts or challenges within the team: Sales Engineers should practice active listening, stay calm under pressure, and seek** a solution that works for everyone involved. This can be done by approaching conflicts with a solution-focused mindset, remaining calm and composed, and seeking out the input and feedback of all team members.

5. **To overcome not taking responsibility for team successes and failures:** Sales Engineers should take ownership of their actions and decisions and actively contribute to the team's goals and objectives. This can be done by setting clear and measurable goals, holding oneself accountable for results, and actively seeking out opportunities for improvement and learning. Additionally, reaching out to managers or mentors for support and guidance when setting goals is important.

In conclusion, working well in a team is essential for success as a Sales Engineer. Common mistakes that Sales Engineers may make include not effectively communicating with team members, not actively participating in team meetings, not being willing to help others or share information, not being able to handle conflicts or challenges within the team, and not taking responsibility for team successes and failures. By understanding these mistakes and implementing strategies to overcome them, Sales Engineers can improve their teamwork skills and contribute to their team's success.

THINKING QUESTION

What actions can you take to improve your team's communication, participation, cooperation, conflict resolution, and accountability?

BE ABLE TO MANAGE TIME AND PRIORITIZE EFFECTIVELY.

As a Sales Engineer, managing your time and prioritizing effectively is crucial to success in the sales process. However, it can be easy to fall into common mistakes that lead to poor productivity and efficiency. This chapter will explore the most common mistakes Sales Engineers make when managing time and prioritizing and provide strategies for overcoming these mistakes. By understanding and avoiding these mistakes, Sales Engineers can ensure that their time is being used effectively and that they are working towards achieving their objectives.

Below are the top 5 mistakes Sales Engineers make in managing time and prioritizing work effectively:

1. **Not setting clear and specific goals:** Sales Engineers should set clear and specific goals to ensure that their time is being used effectively and that they are working towards achieving their objectives. Failing to set clear and specific goals can lead to a lack of

direction and focus, negatively impacting productivity and efficiency.

2. **Not creating a schedule or to-do list:** Sales Engineers should create a schedule or to-do list to keep track of their tasks and deadlines and ensure they are using their time effectively. Failing to create a schedule or to-do list can lead to a lack of organization and focus, negatively impacting productivity and efficiency.

3. **Not prioritizing tasks:** Sales Engineers should prioritize their tasks to ensure that they are working on the most important tasks first. Failing to prioritize tasks can lead to procrastination and a lack of productivity, as well as an inability to meet deadlines.

4. **Not being able to manage distractions:** Sales Engineers should be able to manage distractions to stay focused and productive. Failing to manage distractions can lead to a lack of concentration and productivity, as well as an inability to meet deadlines.

How to overcome these top 5 mistakes:

1. **To overcome not setting clear and specific goals:** Sales Engineers should take the time to identify their overall objectives and then break them down into smaller, more manageable goals. They should also set specific, measurable, and attainable targets for each goal and regularly review their progress to ensure they are on track to achieve them. Additionally, it's important to

seek support and guidance from managers, mentors, coworkers, or friends when setting and working towards goals.

2. **To overcome not creating a schedule or to-do list:** Sales Engineers should develop a daily or weekly schedule that outlines their tasks and deadlines. They should also create a to-do list that prioritizes the most important tasks and use time management tools such as calendars, reminders, and productivity apps to stay organized and on top of their tasks.

3. **To overcome not prioritizing tasks:** Sales Engineers should use the Eisenhower Matrix, a prioritization method that helps to identify which tasks are urgent and important and focus on completing those first. The matrix divides tasks into four categories:

   a. Urgent and important (tasks that require immediate attention)

   b. Important but not urgent (important tasks that can be scheduled)

   c. Urgent but not important (tasks that can be delegated)

   d. Not urgent or important (tasks that can be eliminated).

By using this matrix, Sales Engineers can focus on the most important tasks that must be completed first. It's also important to be mindful of their energy levels and work on tasks that align with their most productive hours. To help understand the concept, an example of the Eisenhower matrix is often represented as a grid with four quadrants, each representing one of the above-mentioned categories.

4. **To overcome not being able to manage distractions:** Sales Engineers should use techniques such as the Pomodoro Technique, which involves working in short, focused bursts and taking regular breaks to recharge. They should also consider using noise-canceling headphones, turning off notifications, and working in a dedicated workspace to minimize distractions. However, it's important to note that blocking off all notifications can lead to missing important messages, so Sales Engineers should find a balance that works for them. To ensure important messages are not missed while minimizing distractions, they can block off specific time slots on their calendar, during which they are heads-down and focused, and make these time slots visible to others. This way, colleagues and clients will know when the Sales Engineer is available for interruptions and when they are focusing on important tasks.

In conclusion, managing time and prioritizing effectively are crucial for Sales Engineers to succeed. Common mistakes include not setting clear and specific goals, not creating a schedule or to-do list, not prioritizing tasks, not being able to manage distractions, and not being able to manage time effectively. By identifying these mistakes and implementing strategies to overcome them, Sales Engineers can improve their productivity and efficiency and ultimately close more sales.

THINKING QUESTION

How can you improve your time management and prioritization skills to ensure that you use your time efficiently and effectively?

CONTINUOUSLY STRIVE TO IMPROVE AND LEARN NEW SKILLS.

As a Sales Engineer, it is important to continuously strive to improve and learn new skills to stay competitive in the industry and excel in your role. However, there can be common mistakes that Sales Engineers make in this area, such as failing to set personal and professional development goals, not taking advantage of training and development opportunities, and not staying informed about industry trends and changes. In this chapter, we will discuss these mistakes and provide strategies to overcome them to continuously improve and excel in your career as a Sales Engineer.

Below are the top 5 mistakes Sales Engineers make about continuous improvement and keeping skills up to date:

1. **Failing to set personal and professional development goals:** Sales Engineers should set personal and professional development goals to improve their skills

and stay competitive in the industry continuously. Failing to set these goals can result in stagnation and a lack of progress in one's career.

2. **Not taking advantage of training and development opportunities:** Sales Engineers should take advantage of training and development opportunities to learn new skills and stay current with industry trends. Failing to do so can result in a lack of knowledge and skills needed to excel in the job.

3. **Not seeking out feedback and constructive criticism:** Sales Engineers should actively seek feedback and constructive criticism to identify improvement areas and gain insights from others. Failing to do so can result in a lack of self-awareness and the ability to improve.

4. **Not staying informed about industry trends and changes:** Sales Engineers should stay informed about industry trends and changes to stay competitive and to be able to adapt to new market conditions. Failing to stay informed can result in a lack of understanding of the industry and the ability to adapt to new market conditions.

5. **Not being open to new ideas and perspectives:** Sales Engineers should be open to new ideas and perspectives to improve their skills and stay competitive in the industry continuously. Failing to be

open to new ideas can result in a lack of creativity and the ability to adapt to new market conditions.

How to overcome these top 5 mistakes:

1. **To overcome failing to set personal and professional development goals:** Sales Engineers should take the time to identify their strengths and weaknesses, set realistic and measurable goals, and create a plan to achieve them.

2. **To overcome not taking advantage of training and development opportunities:** Sales Engineers should actively seek out and take advantage of opportunities for learning and skill development, whether through in-house training programs, workshops, or online courses.

3. **To overcome not seeking out feedback and constructive criticism:** Sales Engineers should actively seek feedback from colleagues, supervisors, and clients and be open to receiving constructive criticism to improve their skills and performance.

4. **To overcome not staying informed about industry trends and changes:** Sales Engineers should stay informed by reading industry publications, attending conferences and networking events, and participating in professional organizations.

5. **To overcome not being open to new ideas and perspectives:** Sales Engineers should actively seek out

diverse perspectives and be open to new ideas, whether it be through collaboration with colleagues, networking with industry professionals, or exploring new technologies and methodologies.

In conclusion, continuously striving to improve and learn new skills is crucial for Sales Engineers to excel in their roles and stay competitive. Common mistakes in this area include failing to set personal and professional development goals, not taking advantage of training and development opportunities, not seeking out feedback and constructive criticism, not staying informed about industry trends and changes, and not being open to new ideas and perspectives. It's important to remember that continuous learning and self-improvement should be lifelong processes.

THINKING QUESTION

What steps can I take to continuously improve and learn new skills in my role as a Sales Engineer?

ONE FINAL THOUGHT

I trust you have enjoyed this book. As you progress, I wish you success and suggest that you keep in mind…..

"The best way to predict the future is to create it." - Abraham Lincoln: Take control of your future by being proactive and creating the desired outcomes.

"Whether you think you can, or you think you can't - you're right." - Henry Ford: Your mindset and attitude can greatly affect your ability to succeed.

"Sales are contingent upon the attitude of the salesman, not the attitude of the prospect." - W. Clement Stone: Having a positive attitude and mindset as a Sales Engineer can greatly impact the success of the sale.

"A goal without a plan is just a wish." - Antoine de Saint-Exupéry: Having a clear plan and strategy to achieve success as a Sales Engineer.

"The only way to do great work is to love what you do." - Steve Jobs: Find passion and enjoyment in their work, as it leads to a higher level of motivation and success.